Word  Bird's™

Valentine's Day
Words

sweetheart

Roses are red.
Violets are blue.
Sugar is sweet.
So are you!

Published in the United States of America by The Child's World®, Inc.
PO Box 326
Chanhassen, MN 55317-0326
800-599-READ
www.childsworld.com

Project Manager Mary Berendes
Editor Katherine Stevenson, Ph.D.
Designer Ian Butterworth

Library of Congress Cataloging-in-Publication Data
Moncure, Jane Belk.
Word Bird's Valentine's Day words / by Jane Belk Moncure.
p. cm.
ISBN 1-56766-629-9 (alk. paper)
1. Vocabulary—Juvenile literature. 2. Valentine's Day—Juvenile literature.
[1. Vocabulary. 2. Valentine's Day. 3. Holidays.]
I.Title: Valentine words. II. Title.
PE1449 .M5338 2001
428.1—dc21
00-010887

Word Bird's™

Valentine's Day Words

by Jane Belk Moncure

illustrated by Chris McEwan

Word Bird made a…

word house.

"I will put Valentine's Day words in my house," said Word Bird.

Word Bird put in these words:

I Love You

FEBRUARY

1	2	3	4	5	6	7
8	9	10	11	12	13	14
15	16	17	18	19	20	21
22	23	24	25	26	27	28

February 14

To:
My Teacher

Valentine's Day

paper hearts

How to make
a heart.

hug   kiss
sweetheart
Be mine.
I love you.

I Love You

valentine words

valentines

valentine tree

Roses are red.
Violets are blue.
Sugar is sweet.
So are you!

valentine verse

valentine post office

valentine puppets

valentine hats

King of Hearts

Come to our
Valentine's
Day party.

Queen of Hearts

candy hearts

pink lemonade

Valentine's Day party

valentine mail

"I love you."

Can you read these Valentine's

February
14

valentine tree

Valentine's
Day

valentine
verse

paper
hearts

valentine
post office

valentine
words

valentine
puppets

valentines

valentine
hats

Day words with Word Bird?

 King of Hearts

 Valentine's Day party

 Queen of Hearts

valentine mail

candy hearts

"I love you."

pink lemonade

You can make a Valentine's Day word house. You can put Word Bird's words in your house and read them, too.

Can you think of other Valentine's Day words to put in your word house?